The Very Best of ANON.

Other Titles from Macmillan

DON'T PANIC!
100 poems to save your life
chosen by Fiona Waters

I REMEMBER, I REMEMBER
poems about the magic of childhood
chosen by Brian Moses

CHRISTMAS POEMS
chosen by Gaby Morgan

The VERY BEST OF ANON.

poems edited by John Foster

MACMILLAN CHILDREN'S BOOKS

First published 2004 by Macmillan Children's Books
a division of Macmillan Publishers Limited
20 New Wharf Road, London N1 9RR
Basingstoke and Oxford
www.panmacmillan.com

Associated companies throughout the world

ISBN 1 405 02053 9

1 3 5 7 9 8 6 4 2

A CIP catalogue record for this book is available from
the British Library.

Typeset by Nigel Hazle
Printed and bound in China

Contents

Seven for a Secret

Who Ever Sausage a Thing?

Look Out, Stomach!

I Had a Little Nut Tree

Ladles and Jellyspoons

Mary Had a Crocodile

As I Walked Out One Night

The Way to the Zoo

Pot Luck

Christmas Crackers

Lettuce Marry

Order in the Court

Seven for a Secret

Seven for a Secret

Seven blackbirds in a tree,
Count them and see what they be.
One for sorrow
Two for joy
Three for a girl
Four for a boy;
Five for silver
Six for gold
Seven for a secret
That's never told.

The Key of the Kingdom

This is the key of the kingdom:
In that kingdom there is a city.
In that city there is a town.
In that town there is a street.
In that street there is a lane.
In that lane there is a yard.
In that yard there is a house.
In that house there is a room.
In that room there is a bed.
On that bed there is a basket.
In that basket there are some flowers.

Flowers in a basket.
Basket on the bed.
Bed in the room.
Room in the house.
House in the yard.
Yard in the lane.
Lane in the street.
Street in the town.
Town in the city.
City in the kingdom.
Of the kingdom this is the key.

I Live in the city

I live in the city, yes I do,
I live in the city, yes I do,
I live in the city, yes I do,
Made by human hands.

Black hands, white hands, yellow and brown
All together built this town,
Black hands, white hands, yellow and brown
All together made the wheels go round.

Black hands, brown hands, yellow and white
Built the buildings tall and bright,
Black hands, brown hands, yellow and white
Filled them all with shining light.

Black hands, white hands, brown and tan
Milled the flour and cleaned the pan,
Black hands, white hands, brown and tan
The working woman and the working man.

I live in the city, yes I do,
I live in the city, yes I do,
I live in the city, yes I do,
Made by human hands.

I Asked the Little Boy Who Cannot See

I asked the little boy who cannot see,
'And what is colour like?'
'Why, green,' said he,
'Is like the rustle when the wind blows through
The forest; running water, that is blue;
And red is like a trumpet sound; and pink
Is like the smell of roses; and I think
That purple must be like a thunderstorm;
And yellow is like something soft and warm;
And white is a pleasant stillness when you lie
And dream.'

The Darkening Garden

Where have all the colours gone?

Red of roses, green of grass,
Brown of tree-trunk, gold of cowslip,
Pink of poppy, blue of cornflower,
Who among you saw them pass?

They have gone to make the sunset:

Broidered on the western sky,
All the colours of our garden,
Woven into a lovely curtain,
Over the bed where Day doth die.

Banyan Tree

Moonshine tonight, come mek me dance and sing,
Moonshine tonight, come mek me dance and sing,
Me deh rock so, yu deh rock so, under banyan tree,
Me deh rock so, yu deh rock so, under banyan tree.

Ladies mek curtsy, an gentlemen mek bow,
Ladies mek curtsy, an gentlemen mek bow,
Me deh rock so, yu deh rock so, under banyan tree,
Me deh rock so, yu deh rock so, under banyan tree.

Den we join hans an dance around an roun,
Den we join hans an dance around an roun,
Me deh rock so, yu deh rock so, under banyan tree,
Me deh rock so, yu deh rock so, under banyan tree.

Lullaby

Hush, little baby, don't say a word,
Papa's going to buy you a mocking bird.

If the mocking bird won't sing,
Papa's going to buy you a diamond ring.

If the diamond ring turns to brass,
Papa's going to buy you a looking glass.

If the looking-glass gets broke,
Papa's going to buy you a billy-goat.

If that billy-goat runs away,
Papa's going to buy you another today.

Star Wish

Star light, star bright,
First star I see tonight,
Wish I may,
Wish I might,
Have the wish I wish tonight.

The Song of the Stars

We are the stars which sing,
We sing with our light;
We are the birds of fire,
We fly over the sky.
Our light is a voice;
We make a road for spirits,
For the spirits to pass over.
Among us are three hunters
Who chase a bear;
There never was a time
When they were not hunting.
We look down on the mountains.
This is the Song of the Stars.

Shine Out Fair Sun

Shine out fair sun, with all your heat,
Show all your thousand-coloured light!
Black Winter freezes to his sea;
The grey wolf howls he does so bite;
Crookt Age on three knees creeps the street;
The boneless fish close quaking lies
And eats for cold his aching feet;
The stars in icicles arise:
Shine out, and make this winter night
Our beauty's Spring, our Prince of light.

Farewell

Thy journey be auspicious; may the breeze,
Gentle and soothing, fan thy cheek; may lakes
All bright with lily cups delight thine eye,
The sunbeam's heat be cooled by shady trees,
The dust beneath thy feet the pollen be
Of lotuses.

Time

Time is too slow for those who wait,
too swift for those who fear,
too long for those who grieve,
too short for those who rejoice,
but for those who love, time is eternity.

children

If children live with criticism
  they learn to condemn

If children live with hostility
  they learn to fight

If children live with ridicule
  they learn to be shy

If children live with shame
  they learn to feel guilty

If children live with tolerance
  they learn to be patient

If children live with encouragement
  they learn confidence

If children live with praise
  they learn to appreciate

If children live with fairness
  they learn justice

If children live with security
  they learn to have faith

If children live with approval
  they learn to like themselves

If children live with acceptance and friendship
  they learn to find love in the world

I'm Glad

I'm glad the sky is painted blue,
And earth is painted green,
With such a lot of nice fresh air
All sandwiched in between.

Yoruba Poem

Enjoy the earth gently
Enjoy the earth gently
For if the earth is spoiled
It cannot be repaired
Enjoy the earth gently

Lines by a Humanitarian

Be lenient to lobsters, and ever kind to crabs,
And be not disrespectful to cuttlefish or dabs;

Chase on the Cochin-China, chaff not the ox obese
And babble not of feather-beds in company with
    geese.

Be tender with the tadpole, and let the limpet thrive,
Be merciful to mussels, don't skin your eels alive;

When talking to a turtle, don't mention calipee –
Be always kind to animals wherever you may be.

Calipee is turtle soup.

The Donkey

I saw a donkey
One day old,
His head was too big
For his neck to hold;
His legs were shaky
And long and loose,
They rocked and staggered
And weren't much use.

He tried to gambol
And frisk a bit,
But he wasn't quite sure
Of the trick of it.
His queer little coat
Was soft and grey,
And curled at his neck
In a lovely way.

His face was wistful
And left no doubt
That he felt life needed
Some thinking about.
So he blundered round
In venturesome quest,
And then lay flat
On the ground to rest.

He looked so little
And weak and slim,
I prayed the world
Might be good to him.

'I,' said the Donkey

'I,' said the donkey, all shaggy and brown,
'Carried his mother all into the town,
Carried her uphill carried her down.
I,' said the donkey, all shaggy and brown.

'I,' said the cow, with spots of red,
'Gave him hay for to rest his head,
Gave a manger for his bed.
I,' said the cow, with spots of red.

'I,' said the sheep, with twisted horn,
'Gave my wool for to keep him warm,
Gave my coat on Christmas morn.
I,' said the sheep with twisted horn.

'I,' said the dove from the rafters high,
'Cooed him to sleep with a lullaby,
Cooed him to sleep my mate and I.
I,' said the dove from the rafters high.

Hindu Poem

Sky so bright
Blue and light
Stars – how many have you?
Countless stars
Countless times
Shall our God be praised now.
Forest green
Cool, serene,
Leaves – how many have you?
Countless leaves
Countless times
Shall our God be praised now.

I Believe

I believe,
I believe in the sun
even where when it is not shining.
I believe in love
even when I cannot feel it.
I believe in God
even when God is silent.

Gaelic Blessing

Deep peace of the running wave to you.
Deep peace of the flowing air to you.
Deep peace of the quiet air to you.
Deep peace of the shining stars to you.
Deep peace of the Son of Peace to you.

The Easterner's Prayer

I pray the prayer the Easterners do –
May the peace of Allah abide with you!
Wherever you stay wherever you go
May the beautiful palms of Allah grow,
Through days of labour and nights of rest,
The love of good Allah make you blest.
So I touch my heart as Easterners do –
May the peace of Allah abide with you!
Salaam Alaikum
(Peace be unto you)

Who Ever Sausage a Thing?

Who Ever Sausage a Thing?

One day a boy went walking
And went into a store;
He bought a pound of sausages
And laid them on the floor.

The boy began to whistle
A merry little tune –
And all the little sausages
Danced around the room.

I Went to the Pictures
Tomorrow

I went to the pictures tomorrow
I took a front seat at the back,
I fell from the pit to the gallery
And broke a front bone in my back.
A lady she gave me some chocolate,
I ate it and gave it her back.
I phoned for a taxi and walked it,
And that's why I never came back.

A Bite of Geography

Long-legged Italy
Kicked poor Sicily
Into the middle of the Mediterranean Sea.
Austria was Hungary,
Took a bit of Turkey,
Dipped it in Greece,
Fried it in Japan,
And ate it off China.

Stately Verse

If Mary goes far out to sea,
By wayward breezes fanned,
I'd like to know – can you tell me? –
Just where would Maryland?

If Tenny went high up in air
And looked o'er land and lea,
Looked here and there and everywhere,
Pray what would Tennessee?

I looked out of the window and
Saw Orry on the lawn;
He's not there now, and who can tell
Just where has Oregon?

Two girls were quarrelling one day
With garden tools, and so
I said, 'My dears, let Mary rake
And just let Idaho.'

A friend of mine lived in a flat
With half a dozen boys;
When he fell ill I asked him why.
He said, 'I'm Illinois.'

An English lady had a steed.
She called him 'Ighland Bay.
She rode for exercise and thus
Rhode Island every day.

MISSISSIPPI Said to Missouri

Mississippi said to Missouri,
'If I put on my New Jersey
What will Delaware?'
Virginia said, 'Alaska.'

One Old Oxford Ox

One old Oxford ox opening oysters,
Two teetotums totally tired trying to trot to Tadbury;
Three tall tigers tippling tuppenny tea;
Four fine foxes fanning fainting friars;
Five flighty flibbertigibbets foolishly fishing for flies;
Six sportsmen shooting snipes;
Seven Severn salmons swallowing shrimps;
Eight Englishmen eagerly examining Europe;
Nine nimble noblemen nibbling noodles;
Ten tinkers tinkling upon ten tin tinderboxes with ten
    ten-penny tacks;
Eleven elephants elegantly equipped;
Twelve talkative tailors trimming tartan trousers.

A Famous Painter

A famous painter
Met his death
Because he couldn't
Draw his breath.

Coffin

It was a cough
  that carried her off.
It was a coffin
  they carried her off in.

Miles' Stone

This tombstone is a milestone.
Ha! How so?
Because beneath lies Miles, who's
Miles below.

As the Witch said to the Skeleton

WITCH: 'Come on out of that cupboard.'
SKELETON: 'I haven't got the face to.'

WITCH: 'Oh, come on. There's a dance down the road. Why don't you go?'
SKELETON: 'I haven't any body to go with.'

WITCH: 'Don't you know *anyone*?'
SKELETON: 'No, I haven't got a single ghoul-friend.'

WITCH: 'Well, you needn't sound so sorry for yourself.'
SKELETON: 'Well, I've lost my voice; among other things I haven't got a leg to stand on.'

WITCH: 'I suppose you were trying to throw
   yourself off that cliff yesterday?'
SKELETON: 'No, I hadn't got the guts.'

WITCH: 'Scared, eh?'
SKELETON: 'Me scared? You couldn't make *me*
   jump out of my skin if you tried.'

WITCH: 'I don't know why I bother with you –
   you're just a bone-idle old bonehead.'
SKELETON: 'That's right.'

Moses

Moses supposes his toeses are roses,
But Moses supposes erroneously;
For nobody's toeses are posies of roses
As Moses supposes his toeses to be.

I'm Thor

The thunder god went for a ride
Upon his favourite filly
    'I'm Thor,' he cried,
    And the horse replied,
'You forgot your thaddle, thilly.'

A Puzzle

It has always been a puzzle to me
What sailors sow when they 'plough' the sea.
Does coffee go with the 'roll' of a drum?
And why is a 'speaking' likeness dumb?
What was it that made the window 'blind'?
Whose picture is put in a 'frame of mind'?
When a storm is 'brewing' what does it brew?
Does the 'foot' of a mountain wear a shoe?
Can a drink be got from a 'tap' on the door?
Does the 'edge' of the water cut the shore?
How long does it take to 'hatch' a plot?
Has a 'school' of herring a tutor or not?
Have you ever penned a 'volume' of smoke?

Can butter be made from the 'cream' of a joke?
Who is it fixes the 'teeth' in a gale?
To a king who 'reigns' why shout 'O Hail'?
Can you fasten the door with a 'lock' of hair?
Did a 'biting' wind ever bite you and where?
Who is it paints the 'signs' of the times?
Does the moon change her 'quarters' for nickels and
   dimes?
What tunes do you 'play' on your feelings, pray?
And who is it mends the 'break' of day?
And say – I'll admit this is quite absurd –
When you 'drop' a remark, do you 'break' your
   word?

Hints on Pronunciation for Foreigners

I take it you already know
Of tough and bough and cough and dough?
Others may stumble, but not you
On hiccough, thorough, laugh and through?
Well done! And now you wish perhaps
To learn of these familiar traps?

Beware of heard, a dreadful word,
That looks like beard and sounds like bird,
And dead: it's said like bed, not bead,
For Goodness' sake, don't call it deed!
Watch out for meat and great and threat,
They rhyme with suite and straight and debt.

A moth is not a moth in mother
Nor both in bother, broth in brother,
And here is not a match for there,
Nor dear and fear for bear and pear,
And then there's does and rose and lose –
Just look them up: and goose and choose,

And cork and front and word and ward
And font and front and word and sword.
And do and go and thwart and cart –
Come, come, I've hardly made a start!
A dreadful language? Man Alive,
I'd mastered it when I was five.

Life Is Butter

Life is butter, life is butter;
Melancholy flower, melancholy flower;
Life is but a melon, life is but a melon;
Cauliflower, cauliflower.

Sign of an Early Spring

'Tis dog's delight to bark and bite
And little birds to sing,
And if you sit on a red-hot brick
It's a sign of an early spring.

The Joke

The joke you just told isn't funny one bit.
It's pointless and dull, wholly lacking in wit.
It's old and stale, it's beginning to smell!
Besides, it's the one I was going to tell.

Look Out, Stomach

Look Out, Stomach

Through the teeth
And past the gums,
Look out, stomach,
Here it comes!

School Dinners

If you stay to school dinners
Better throw them aside;
A lot of kids didn't,
A lot of kids died.
The meat is iron,
The spuds are steel;
If the first course don't get you,
Then the afters will.

Apple Pie

A was an Apple Pie
B bit it, C cut it, D dealt it,
E enjoyed it, F fought for it,
G got it, H hoped for it,
I inquired about it,
J jumped on it, K kept it,
L longed for it, M mourned for it,
N nodded at it, O opened it,
P peered in it, Q quartered it,
R ran for it, S sat on it, T took it,
U upset it, V viewed it, W wanted it,
X crossed it, Y yearned for it,
And Z put it in his pocket, and said,
'Well done!'

There Was a Young Lad of St Just

There was a young lad of St Just
Who ate apple pie till he bust.
   It wasn't the fru-it
   That caused him to do it,
What finished him off was the crust.

The Greedy Man

The greedy man is he who sits
And bites bits out of plates,
Or else takes up the almanac
And gobbles all the dates.

Mary

Mary ate jam,
Mary ate jelly,
Mary went home
With a pain in her –
Now don't get excited
Don't be misled
Mary went home
With a pain in her head.

On Top of Spaghetti

On top of spaghetti, all covered with cheese,
I lost my poor meatball when somebody sneezed.

It rolled off the table, and on to the floor,
And then my poor meatball rolled out of the door.

It rolled into the garden, and under a bush,
And then my poor meatball was nothing but mush.

The mush was as tasty, as tasty can be,
And early next summer, it grew into a tree.

The tree was all covered, with beautiful moss,
It grew lovely meatballs and tomato sauce.

So if you eat spaghetti, all covered with cheese,
Hold on to your meatball, and don't ever sneeze.

I Eat My Peas With Honey

I eat my peas with honey,
I've done it all my life.
It makes the peas taste funny,
But it keeps them on the knife.

The Boy Stood in the Supper-Room

The boy stood in the supper-room
  Whence all but he had fled;
He'd eaten seven pots of jam
  And he was gorged with bread.

'Oh, one more crust before I bust!'
  He cried in accents wild;
He licked the plates, he sucked the spoons –
  He was a vulgar child.

There came a burst of thunder-sound –
  The boy – oh! Where was he?
Ask of the maid who mopped him up.
  The bread crumbs and the tea.

Look Out, Stomach!

On Nevski Bridge

On Nevski Bridge a Russian stood
Chewing his beard for lack of food.
He said, 'It's tough this stuff to eat
But a darn sight better than shredded wheat.'

I Had a Little Nut Tree

I Had a Little Nut Tree

I had a little nut tree,
Nothing would it bear
But a silver nutmeg
And a golden pear;
The King of Spain's daughter
Came to visit me,
And all for the sake of
My little nut tree.
I skipped over water,
I danced over sea,
And all the birds in the air
Couldn't catch me.

What are Little Boys Made of?

What are little boys made of, made of?
What are little boys made of?
  Frogs and snails
  And puppy-dogs' tails,
That's what little boys are made of.

What are little girls made of, made of?
What are little girls made of?
  Sugar and spice
  And all things nice,
That's what little girls are made of.

Nobody Loves Me

Nobody loves me,
Everybody hates me,
I think I'll go and eat worms.

Big fat squishy ones,
Little thin skinny ones,
See how they wriggle and squirm.

Bite their heads off.
'Schlurp!' they're lovely,
Throw their tails away.

Nobody knows
How big I grows
On worms three times a day.

A Frog He Would A-Wooing Go

A Frog he would a-wooing go,
   Heigho, says Rowley,
Whether his mother would let him or no,
With a rowley, powley, gammon and spinach,
   Heigho, says Anthony Rowley!

So off he sets in his opera hat,
   Heigho, says Rowley,
And on the road he met with a rat,
With a rowley, powley, gammon and spinach,
   Heigho, says Anthony Rowley!

'Pray, Mr Rat, will you go with me,'
   Heigho, says Rowley,
'Kind Mrs Mousey for to see?'
With a rowley, powley, gammon and spinach,
   Heigho, says Anthony Rowley!

When they come to the door of Mousey's
    Hall,
    Heigho, says Rowley,
They gave a loud knock, and they gave a
    loud call.
With a rowley, powley, gammon and spinach,
    Heigho, says Anthony Rowley!

'Pray Mrs Mouse, are you within?'
    Heigho, says Rowley,
'Oh yes, kind sirs, I'm sitting to spin.'
With a rowley, powley, gammon and spinach,
    Heigho, says Anthony Rowley!

'Pray Mrs Mouse, will you give us some
    beer?'
    Heigho, says Rowley,
'For Froggy and I are fond of good cheer.'
With a rowley, powley, gammon and spinach,
    Heigho, says Anthony Rowley!

'Pray, Mr Frog, will you give us a song?'
  Heigho, says Rowley,
'But let it be something that's not very
  long.'
With a rowley, powley, gammon and spinach,
  Heigho, says Anthony Rowley!

But while they were all a-merry-making,
  Heigho, says Rowley,
A cat and her kittens came tumbling in.
With a rowley, powley, gammon and spinach,
  Heigho, says Anthony Rowley.

The cat she seized the rat by the crown;
  Heigho, says Rowley,
The kittens they pulled the little mouse
  down.
With a rowley, powley, gammon and spinach,
  Heigho, says Anthony Rowley.

This put Mr Frog in a terrible fright,
  Heigho, says Rowley,
He took up his hat, and wished them
  goodnight.
With a rowley, powley, gammon and spinach,
  Heigho, says Anthony Rowley.

But as Froggy was crossing over a brook,
  Heigho, says Rowley,
A lily-white duck came and swallowed him
  up.
With a rowley, powley, gammon and spinach,
  Heigho, says Anthony Rowley.

I Had a Little Nut Tree 59

Monday's Child

Monday's child is fair of face,
Tuesday's child is full of grace,
Wednesday's child is full of woe,
Thursday's child has far to go,
Friday's child is loving and giving,
Saturday's child works hard for a living,
And the child that is born on the Sabbath day
Is bonny and blithe, and good and gay.

Solomon Grundy

Solomon Grundy
Born on a Monday,
Christened on Tuesday,
Married on Wednesday,
Took ill on Thursday,
Worse on Friday,
Died on Saturday,
Buried on Sunday.
This is the end
Of Solomon Grundy.

Soldier, Soldier, Will You Marry Me?

Oh soldier, soldier, will you marry me,
With your musket, fife, and drum?
Oh, no, pretty maid, I cannot marry you,
For I have no coat to put on.

Then away she went to the tailor's shop
As fast as legs could run,
And bought him one of the very very best
And the soldier put it on.

Oh soldier, soldier, will you marry me,
With your musket, fife, and drum?
Oh no, pretty maid, I cannot marry you,
For I have no shoes to put on.

Then away she went to the cobbler's shop
As fast as legs could run,
And bought him a pair of the very very best,
And the soldier put them on.

Oh soldier, soldier, will you marry me,
With your musket, fife, and drum?
Oh no, pretty maid, I cannot marry you,
For I have no socks to put on.

Then away she went to the sock-maker's shop
As fast as legs could run,
And bought him a pair of the very very best,
And the soldier put them on.

Oh soldier, soldier, will you marry me,
With your musket, fife, and drum?
Oh no, pretty maid, I cannot marry you,
For I have no hat to put on.

Then away she went to the hatter's shop
As fast as legs could run,
And bought him one of the very very best,
And the soldier put them on.

Oh soldier, soldier, will you marry me,
With your musket, fife, and drum?
Oh no, pretty maid, I cannot marry you,
For I have a wife at home.

Bobby Shaftoe

Bobby Shaftoe's gone to sea,
Silver buckles at his knee;
He'll come back and marry me,
      Bonny Bobby Shaftoe.

Bobby Shaftoe's bright and fair,
Combing down his yellow hair,
He's my ain for evermair,
      Bonny Bobby Shaftoe.

Bobby Shaftoe's tall and slim,
He's always dressed so neat and trim,
The ladies they all keek at him,
      Bonny Bobby Shaftoe.

Bobby Shaftoe's getten a bairn
For to dandle in his arm;
In his arm and on his knee,
      Bonny Bobby Shaftoe.

Thirty Days Hath September

Thirty days hath September,
April, June and November.
All the rest have thirty-one,
Except February alone,
Which has four and twenty-four
Till leap year gives it one day more.

For Want of a Nail

For want of a nail, the shoe was lost;
For want of the shoe, the horse was lost;
For want of the horse, the rider was lost;
For want of the rider, the battle was lost;
For want of the battle, the kingdom was lost;
And all for the want of a horseshoe nail.

Simple Simon

Simple Simon met a pieman,
Going to the fair;
Says Simple Simon to the pieman,
'Let me taste your ware.'

Says the pieman to Simple Simon,
'Show me first your penny,'
Says Simple Simon to the pieman,
'Indeed I have not any.'

Simple Simon went a-fishing
For to catch a whale;
All the water he could find
Was in his mother's pail!

Simple Simon went to look
If plums grew on a thistle;
He pricked his fingers very much,
Which made poor Simon whistle.

He went to catch a dicky bird,
And thought he could not fail,
Because he had a little salt,
To put upon its tail.

He went for water with a sieve,
But soon it ran all through;
And now poor Simple Simon
Bids you all adieu.

The North Wind Doth Blow

The north wind doth blow,
And we shall have snow,
And what will the robin do then,
      poor thing?
  He'll sit in a barn,
   And keep himself warm,
And hide his head under his wing,
      poor thing!

The north wind doth blow,
And we shall have snow,
And what will the swallow do then,
      poor thing?
  Oh, do you not know
  That he's off long ago,
To a country where he will find spring,
      poor thing!

The north wind doth blow,
And we shall have snow,
And what will the dormouse do then,
      poor thing?
  Roll'd up like a ball,

In his nest snug and small,
He'll sleep till warm weather comes in,
        poor thing!

The north wind doth blow,
And we shall have snow,
And what will the honeybee do then,
        poor thing?
    In his hive he will stay
    Till the cold is away,
And then he'll come out in the spring,
        poor thing!

The north wind doth blow,
And we shall have snow,
And what will the children do then,
        poor things?
    When lessons are done,
    They must skip, jump and run,
Until they have made themselves warm,
        Poor things!

Adam and Eve and Pinch-Me

Adam and Eve and Pinch-me
Went down to the river to bathe.
Adam and Eve were drowned –
Who do you think was saved?

A Tree Toad Loved a She-toad

A tree toad loved a she-toad
   That lived up in a tree.
She was a three-toed tree toad
   But a two-toed toad was he.
The two-toed toad tried to win
   The she-toad's friendly nod,
For the two-toed toad loved the ground
   On which the three-toed toad trod.
But no matter how the two-toed tree toad tried,
   He could not please her whim.
In her tree-toad bower,
   With her three-toed power
The she-toad vetoed him.

There Was an Old Lady

There was an old lady who swallowed a fly.
Poor old lady, she swallowed a fly.
I don't know why she swallowed a fly.
Perhaps she'll die.

There was an old lady who swallowed a fly.
Poor old lady, she swallowed a spider.
It squirmed and wriggled and turned inside her.
She swallowed the spider to catch the fly.
I don't know why she swallowed a fly.
Perhaps she'll die.

There was an old lady who swallowed a fly.
Poor old lady, she swallowed a bird.
How absurd! She swallowed a bird.
She swallowed the bird to catch the spider,
She swallowed the spider to catch the fly.
I don't know why she swallowed a fly.
Perhaps she'll die.

There was an old lady who swallowed a fly.
Poor old lady, she swallowed a cat.
Think of that! She swallowed a cat.
She swallowed the cat to catch the bird.
She swallowed the bird to catch the spider,
She swallowed the spider to catch the fly.
I don't know why she swallowed a fly.
Perhaps she'll die.

There was an old lady who swallowed a fly.
Poor old lady, she swallowed a dog.
She went the whole hog when she swallowed the dog.
She swallowed the dog to catch the cat,
She swallowed the cat to catch the bird,
She swallowed the bird to catch the spider.
She swallowed the spider to catch the fly,
I don't know why she swallowed a fly.
Perhaps she'll die.

There was an old lady who swallowed a fly.
Poor old lady, she swallowed a cow.
I don't know how she swallowed the cow.
She swallowed the cow to catch the dog,
She swallowed the dog to catch the cat,
She swallowed a cat to catch the bird.
She swallowed the bird to catch the spider,
She swallowed the spider to catch the fly,
I don't know why she swallowed a fly.
Perhaps she'll die.

Poor old lady, she swallowed a horse.
She died, of course.

The Cock Crows in the Morn

The cock crows in the morn
To tell us to rise,
And he that lies late
Will never be wise:
For early to bed,
And early to rise,
Is the way to be healthy
And wealthy and wise.

Dance to your Daddy

Dance to your daddy,
My little babby,
Dance to your daddy,
My little lamb;

You shall have a fishy
In a little dishy,
You shall have a fishy
When the boat comes in.

Baby shall have an apple,
Baby shall have a plum,
Baby shall have a rattle
When Daddy comes home.

Who Killed Cock Robin?

Who killed Cock Robin?
I, said the Sparrow,
With my bow and arrow,
I killed Cock Robin.

Who saw him die?
I, said the Fly,
With my little eye,
I saw him die.

Who saw his blood?
I, said the Fish,
With my little dish,
I caught his blood.

Who'll make his shroud?
I, said the Beetle,
With my thread and needle,
I'll make his shroud.

Who'll dig his grave?
I, said the Owl,
With my pick and shovel,
I'll dig his grave.

Who'll be the parson?
I, said the Rook,
With my little book,
I'll be the parson.

Who'll be the clerk
I, said the Lark,
If it's not in the dark,
I'll be the clerk.

Who'll carry the link?
I, said the Linnet,
I'll fetch it in a minute
I'll carry the link.

Who'll be the chief mourner?
I, said the Dove,
I mourn for my love,
I'll be chief mourner.

I Had a Little Nut Tree

Who'll carry the coffin?
I, said the Kite,
If it's not through the night,
I'll carry the coffin.

Who'll bear the pall?
We, said the Wren,
Both the cock and the hen,
We'll bear the pall.

Who'll sing the psalm?
I, said the Thrush,
As she sat on a bush,
I'll sing a psalm.

Who'll toll the bell?
I, said the Bull,
Because I can pull,
So Cock Robin, farewell.

All the birds of the air
Fell-a-sighing and a-sobbing,
When they heard the bell toll
For poor Cock Robin

Clementine

Oh my darling, oh my darling,
Oh my darling Clementine!
Thou are lost and gone forever,
Oh my darling, Clementine.

In a cavern, in a canyon,
Excavating for a mine,
Lived a miner, forty-niner,
And his daughter, Clementine.

Light she was and like a fairy,
And her shoes were number nine,
Herring boxes without topses
Sandals were for Clementine.

Drove she ducklings to the water
Every morning just at nine.
Hit her foot against a splinter,
Fell into the foaming brine.

Saw her lips above the water
Blowing bubbles mighty fine.
But alas! I was no swimmer,
So I lost my Clementine.

How I missed her, how I missed her,
How I missed my Clementine.
But I kissed her little sister
And forgot my Clementine.

Oh my darling, oh my darling,
Oh my darling Clementine!
Thou are lost and gone forever,
Dreadful sorry, Clementine.

Ladles and Jellyspoons

Ladles and Jellyspoons

Ladles and Jellyspoons,
I come before you
To stand behind you
And tell you something
I know nothing about.
Next Thursday
Which is Good Friday
There'll be a Mothers' Meeting
For Fathers only.
Wear your best clothes if you haven't any

And if you can come
Please stay at home.
Admission free
Pay at the door
Take a seat
And sit on the floor.
It makes no difference where you sit
The man in the gallery is sure to spit.

Crazy Days

'Twas midnight on the ocean,
Not a streetcar was in sight;
The sun was shining brightly,
For it rained all day that night.

'Twas a summer day in winter
And snow was raining fast,
As a barefoot boy with shoes on
Stood sitting in the grass.

One Fine Day in the Middle of the Night

One fine day in the middle of the night
Two dead men got up to fight.
Back to back they faced each other,
Drew their swords and shot each other.

.

The Snowman

Once there was a snowman
Stood outside the door
Thought he'd like to come inside
And run around the floor;
Thought he'd like to warm himself
By the firelight red;
Thought he'd like to climb up
On that big white bed.
So he called the North Wind, 'Help me now I pray.
I'm completely frozen, standing here all day.'
So the North Wind came along and blew him in the
    door,
And now there's nothing left of him
But a puddle on the floor!

I Saw

I saw a peacock with a fiery tail
I saw a blazing comet drop down hail
I saw a cloud with ivy circled round
I saw a sturdy oak creep on the ground
I saw an ant swallow up a whale
I saw a raging sea brim full of ale
I saw a Venice glass sixteen foot deep
I saw a well full of men's tears that weep
I saw their eyes all in a flame of fire
I saw a house as big as the moon and
  higher
I saw the sun even in the midst of night
I saw the man that saw this wondrous sight.

As I Was Standing in the Street

As I was standing in the street,
As quiet as could be,
A great big ugly man came up
And tied his horse to me.

On the Bridge

He stood on the bridge at midnight,
Disturbing my sweet repose,
For he was a large mosquito –
And the bridge was the bridge of my nose!

Parking Problem

When Noah sailed the waters blue,
He had his troubles, same as you.
For forty days he drove his ark
Before he found a place to park.

Well, Hardly Ever

Never throw a brick at a drownin' man
Outside a grocery store –
Always throw a bar of soap –
And he'll wash himself ashore.

As I Was Going Out One Day

As I was going out one day
My head fell off and rolled away.
But when I saw that it was gone,
I picked it up and put it on.

And when I got into the street
A fellow cried: 'Look at your feet!'
I looked at them and sadly said:
'I've left them both asleep in bed!'

The Man in the Wilderness

The Man in the Wilderness asked of me
'How many blackberries grow in the sea?'
I answered him as I thought good,
'As many red herrings as grow in the wood.'

The Man in the Wilderness asked me why
His hen could swim and his pig could fly.
I answered him briskly as I thought best,
'Because they were born in a cuckoo's nest.'

The Man in the Wilderness asked me to tell
The sands in the sea and I counted them well.
Says he with a grin, 'And not one more?'
I answered him bravely, 'You go and make sure!'

As I Was Going up the Stair

As I was going up the stair
I met a man who wasn't there.
He wasn't there again today.
Oh, how I wish he'd go away.

An Accident Happened to My Brother Jim

An accident happened to my brother Jim
When somebody threw a tomato at him –
Tomatoes are juicy and don't hurt the skin,
But this one was specially packed in a tin.

Llewelyn Peter James Maguire

Llewelyn Peter James Maguire
Touched a live electric wire.
Back on his heels it sent him rocking –
His language (like the wire) was shocking.

The Optimist

The optimist fell ten storeys
  And at each window bar
He shouted to the folks inside
  'Doing all right so far!'

Doctor Bell

Doctor Bell fell down the well
And broke his collar-bone.
Doctors should attend the sick
And leave the well alone.

Last Night

The Eskimo sleeps on his white bearskin,
And sleeps rather well, I'm told.
Last night I slept in my little bare skin
And caught a terrible cold.

Germ Warfare

I shot a sneeze into the air.
It fell to earth I know not where.
But some time later, so I'm told,
Twenty others caught my cold.

Quick! Quick!

Quick, quick, the cat's been sick.
Where? Where?
Under the chair!
Hasten, hasten, fetch a basin!
Oh, Kate, Kate. You're far too late!
The carpet's in a dreadful state!

I Love to Do My Homework

I love to do my homework
I never miss a day.
I even love the men in white
Who are taking me away.

End of Summer Term

Tonight, tonight, the pillow fight,
Tomorrow's the end of school,
Break the dishes, break the chairs,
Trip the teachers on the stairs.

Four more days and we are free
From the school of misery.
No more pencils, no more books,
No more teachers' grumpy looks!

Mary Had a Crocodile

Mary Had a Crocodile

Mary had a crocodile
That ate a child each day,
But interfering people came
And took her pet away.

Roses Are Red

Roses are red,
Violets are blue.
Onions stink
And so do you!

Mary Had a Little Lamb

Mary had a little lamb,
She ate it with mint sauce,
And everywhere that Mary went
The lamb went too, of course!

Little Jack Horner

Little Jack Horner
Sat in a corner,
Watching the girls go by.
Along came a beauty
And he said, 'Hi, cutie!'
And that's how he got a black eye.

Diddle Diddle Dumpling

Diddle diddle dumpling my son John
Ate a pasty five feet long.
He bit it once, he bit it twice.
Then spat it out! It was full of mice!

Rock-a-bye, Baby

Rock-a-bye, baby,
In the treetop.
Don't you fall out –
It's a very big drop.

Hickory Dickory Dock

Hickory, dickory, dock
Two mice ran up the clock.
The clock struck one –
But the other one got away.

Little Miss Muffet

Little Miss Muffet
Sat on a tuffet
Eating her Irish stew.
Along came a spider
Who sat down beside her
And so she ate him up too.

Mary Had a Little Watch

Mary had a little watch.
She swallowed it one day.
So now she's taking laxatives
To pass the time away.

The Village Burglar

Under the spreading gooseberry bush
The village burglar lies;
The burglar is a hairy man
With whiskers round his eyes.

He goes to church on Sundays;
He hears the parson shout;
He puts a penny in the plate
And takes a shilling out.

As I Walked Out One Night

As I Walked Out One Night

As I walked out one night, it being dark all over,
The moon did show no light I could discover,
Down by a riverside where ships were sailing,
A lonely maid I spied, weeping and bewailing.

I boldly stepped up to her, and asked what grieved
   her,
She made this reply, None could relieve her,
'For my love is pressed,' she cried, 'to cross the ocean,
My mind is like the Sea, always in motion.'

He said, 'My pretty fair maid, mark well my story,
For your true love and I fought for England's glory,
By one unlucky shot we both got parted,
And by the wounds he got, I'm broken hearted.

'He told me before he died, his heart was broken,
He gave me this gold ring, take it for a token, –
"Take this unto my dear, there is no one fairer,
Tell her to be kind and love the bearer."'

Soon as these words he spoke she ran distracted,
Not knowing what he did, nor how she acted,
She ran ashore, her hair showing her anger,
'Young man, you've come too late, for I'll wed no
    stranger.'

Soon as these words she spoke, his love grew stronger,
He flew into her arms, he could wait no longer,
They both sat down and sung, but she sung clearest,
Like a nightingale in spring, 'Welcome home, my
   dearest.'

He sang, 'God bless the wind that blew him over.'
She sang, 'God bless the ship that brought him over.'
They both sat down and sung but she sung clearest,
Like a nightingale in spring, 'Welcome home, my
   dearest.'

Old Man Know-All

Old Man Know-All, he comes around
With his nose in the air, turned away from the
  ground.
His old hair hadn't been combed for weeks.
He said, 'Keep still while Know-All speaks.'

Old Man Know-All's tongue did run.
He knew everything under the sun.
When you knew one thing, he knew more.
He talked enough to make a hearing aid sore.

Old Man Know-All died last week.
He got drowned in the middle of the creek.
The bridge was there and there to stay –
But he knew too much to cross that way.

The Little Boy Who Cried All the Time

Once a little boy, Jack, was, oh! ever so good,
Till he took a strange notion to cry all he could.

So he cried all the day, and he cried all the night,
He cried in the morning, and in the twilight;

He cried till his voice was as hoarse as a crow,
And his mouth grew so large it looked like a great O.

It grew at the bottom, and it grew at the top;
It grew till they thought that it never would stop.

Each day his great mouth grew taller and taller,
And his dear little self grew smaller and smaller.

At last, that same mouth grew so big that – alack! –
It was only a mouth with a border of Jack.

Noise

Billy is blowing his trumpet;
Bertie is banging a tin;
Betty is crying for Mummy
And Bob has pricked Ben with a pin.
Baby is crying out loudly;
He's out on the lawn in his pram.
I am the only one silent
And I've eaten all of the jam.

New Shoes

My shoes are new and squeaky shoes,
They're shiny, creaky shoes,
I wish I had my leaky shoes
That my mother threw away.

I liked my old brown leaky shoes
Much better than these creaky shoes,
These shiny, creaky, squeaky shoes
I've got to wear today.

Mr Nobody

I know a funny little man,
As quiet as a mouse.
He does the mischief that is done
In everybody's house.
Though no one ever sees his face,
Yet one and all agree
That every plate we break, was cracked
By Mr Nobody.

'Tis he who always tears our books,
Who leaves the door ajar.
He picks the buttons from our shirts,
And scatters pins afar.
That squeaking door will always squeak –
For prithee, don't you see?
We leave the oiling to be done
By Mr Nobody.

He puts damp wood upon the fire,
That kettles will not boil:
His are the feet that bring in mud
And all the carpets soil.
The papers that so oft are lost –
Who had them last but he?
There's no one tosses them about
But Mr Nobody.

The finger marks upon the door
By none of us were made.
We never leave the blinds unclosed
To let the curtains fade.
The ink we never spill! The boots
That lying round you see,
Are not our boots – they all belong
To Mr Nobody.

Hinx, Minx

Hinx, minx, the old witch winks,
The fat begins to fry.
No one at home but Jumping Joan,
Father, Mother and I.

Stick, stock, stone dead,
Blind men can't see.
Every knave will have a slave.
Is it you or me?

Alone in the Dark

She has taken out the candle,
She has left me in the dark;
From the window not a glimmer,
From the fireplace not a spark.

I am frightened as I'm lying
All alone here in my bed,
And I've wrapped the clothes as close
As I can around my head.

But what is it makes me tremble?
And why should I fear the gloom?
I am certain there is nothing
In the corners of the room.

The Hairy Toe

Once there was a woman went out to pick beans,
And she found a Hairy Toe.
She took the Hairy Toe home with her,
and that night, when she went to bed,
the wind began to moan and groan.
A way off in the distance
she seemed to hear a voice crying,
'Where's my Hair-r-ry To-o-oe?
Who's got my Hair-r-ry To-o-oe?'

The woman scrooched down,
way down under the covers,
and about that time
the wind appeared to hit the house,

smoosh,

and the old house creaked and cracked
like something was trying to get in.
The voice had come nearer,
almost at the door now,
and it said,
'Where's my Hair-r-ry To-o-oe?
Who's got my Hair-r-ry To-o-oe?'

The woman scrooched further down
under the covers
and pulled them tight around her head.

The wind growled around the house
like some big animal
and r-r-um-umbled
over the chimney.
All at once she heard the door cr-r-a-ack
And Something slipped in
and began to creep over the floor.

The floor went
cre-e-eak, cre-e-eak
at every step that thing took towards her bed.
The woman could almost feel
it bending over her head.
There in an awful voice it said:
'Where's my Hair-r-ry To-o-oe?
Who's got my Hair-r-ry To-o-oe?
You've got it!'

Queen Nefertiti

Spin a coin, spin a coin,
   All fall down;
Queen Nefertiti
   Stalks through the town.

Over the pavements
   Her feet go clack.
Her legs are as tall
   As a chimney stack;

Her fingers flicker
   Like snakes in the air,
The walls split open
   At her green-eyed stare;

Her voice is thin
    As the ghosts of bees;
She will crumble your bones
    She will make your blood freeze.

Spin a coin, spin a coin,
    All fall down,
Queen Nefertiti
    Stalks through the town.

There Was a Man of Double Deed

There was a man of double deed
Who sowed his garden full of seed.
Then the seeds began to grow,
like a garden full of snow.
Then the snow began to melt,
like a ship without a belt.
Then the ship began to sail
like a bird without a tail.
Then the bird began to fly,
like an eagle in the sky.
Then the sky began to roar,
like a lion at the door.
Then the door began to crack,
like a stick across my back.

Then my back began to smart,
like a penknife in my heart.
Then my heart began to bleed,
like a needle full of thread.
Then the thread began to rot,
like a turnip in the pot.
Then the pot began to boil,
like a bottle full of oil.
Then the oil began to settle,
like the water in the kettle.
When the kettle boils no more,
Out goes the man to fight a war.

David and Goliath

Goliath of Gath
With hith helmet of brath
Wath theated one day
Upon the green grath.

When up thkipped thlim David
A thervant of Thaul,
And thaid I will thmite thee
Although I am tho thmall.

Thlim David thkipped down
To the edge of the thtream,
And from it'th thmooth thurface
Five thmooth thtones he took.

He loothened hith corthetth
And thevered hith head,
And all Ithrael thouted –
'Goliath ith dead!'

The Way to the Zoo

The Way to the Zoo

That's the way to the zoo.
That's the way to the zoo.
The monkey house is nearly full
But there's room enough for you.

Menagerie

The porcupine may have his quills,
The elephant his trunk;
But when it comes to common scents,
My money's on the skunk.

If You Should Meet a Crocodile

If you should meet a crocodile,
  Don't take a stick and poke him;
Ignore the welcome in his smile,
  Be careful not to stroke him.
For he sleeps upon the Nile,
  He thinner gets and thinner;
But whene'er you meet a crocodile
  He's ready for his dinner.

The Elephant and Its Trunk

The elephant has a great big trunk;
He never packs it with clothes.
It has no lock and it has no key,
But he takes it wherever he goes.

The Hippopotamus

Consider the poor hippopotamus:
His life is unduly monotonous.
He lives half asleep
At the edge of the deep,
And his face is as big as his bottom is.

Radi

Radi was a circus lion.
Radi was a woman hater.
Radi had a lady trainer.
Radiator.

Old Noah's Ark

Old Noah once he built an ark,
And patched it up with hickory bark.
He anchored it to a great big rock,
And then he began to load his stock.
The animals went in one by one,
The elephant chewing a carroway bun.
The animals went in two by two,
The crocodile and the kangaroo.
The animals went in three by three,
The tall giraffe and the tiny flea.
The animals went in four by four,
The hippopotamus stuck in the door.
The animals went in five by five,
The bees mistook the bear for a hive.
The animals went in six by six,
The monkey was up to his usual tricks.
The animals went in seven by seven,
Said the ant to the elephant, 'Who're ye shov'n?'
The animals went in eight by eight,
Some were early and some were late.
The animals went in nine by nine,
They all formed fours and marched in line.
The animals went in ten by ten,
If you want any more, you can read it again.

I Saw a Ship A-Sailing

I saw a ship a-sailing
   A-sailing on the sea,
And oh but it was laden
   With pretty things for me.

There were comfits in the cabin,
   And apples in the hold;
The sails were made of silk,
   And the masts were all of gold.

The four-and-twenty sailors,
   That stood between the decks,
Were four-and-twenty white mice
   With chains about their necks.

The captain was a duck
   With a packet on his back,
And when the ship began to move
   The captain said Quack! Quack!

Seven Fat Fishermen

Seven fat fishermen,
Sitting side by side
Fished from a bridge,
By the banks of the Clyde.

The first caught a tiddler,
The second caught a crab,
The third caught a winkle,
The fourth caught a dab.

The fifth caught a tadpole,
The sixth caught an eel,
But the seventh, he caught
An old cartwheel.

The Centipede's Dilemma

A centipede was happy quite
Until a frog in fun
Said, 'Pray, which leg comes after which?'
This raised her mind to such a pitch,
She lay distracted in a ditch,
Considering how to run.

A Horse and a Flea

A horse and a flea and three blind mice
Sat on a kerbstone shooting dice.
The horse he slipped and fell on the flea.
The flea said, 'Whoops, there's a horse on me.'

Bug in a Jug

Curious fly,
Vinegary jug.
Slippery edge,
Pickled bug.

Some People Say that Fleas Are Black

Some people say that fleas are black,
But I know it isn't so.
For Mary had a little lamb
Whose fleas was white as snow.

The Firefly

The firefly is a funny bug,
He hasn't any mind;
He blunders all the way through life
With his headlight on behind.

Once Upon a Barren Moor

Once upon a barren moor
There dwelt a bear, also a boar;
The bear could not bear the boar;
The boar thought the bear a bore.
At last the boar could bear no more
The bear that bored him on the moor;
And so one morn the bear he bored –
The bear will bore the boar no more.

The Cow

The cow stood on the hillside,
Its skin as smooth as silk,
It slipped upon a cowslip
And sprained a pint of milk.

I Had a Little Pig

I had a little pig,
I fed him in a trough,
He got so fat
His tail dropped off.
So I got me a hammer,
And I got me a nail,
And I made my little pig
A brand-new tail.

Rabbit

A rabbit raced a turtle,
You know the turtle won;
And Mister Bunny came in late,
A little hot cross bun

I Don't Suppose

I don't suppose
A lobster knows
The proper way
To blow his nose,
Or else perhaps
Beneath the seas,
They have no need
To sniff and sneeze.

Five Little owls

Five little owls in an old elm-tree,
Fluffy and puffy as owls could be,
Blinking and winking with big round eyes
At the big round moon that hung in the skies:
As I passed beneath, I could hear one say,
'There'll be mouse for supper, there will, today!'
Then all of them hooted, 'Tu-whit, Tu-whoo!
Yes, mouse for supper, Hoo hoo, Hoo hoo!'

Montague Michael

Montague Michael
You're much too fat,
You wicked old, wily old,
Well-fed cat.

All night you sleep
On a cushion of silk,
And twice a day
I bring you milk.

And once in a while,
When you catch a mouse,
You're the proudest person
In all the house.

But spoilt as you are,
I tell you, sir,
This dolly is mine
And you can't have her!

St Jerome and His Lion

St Jerome in his study kept a great big cat,
It's always in his pictures, with its feet upon the mat.
Did he give it milk to drink, in a little dish?
When it came to Fridays, did he give it fish?
If I lost my little cat, I'd be sad without it;
I should ask St Jeremy what to do about it;
I should ask St Jeremy, just because of that,
For he's the only saint I know who kept a pussy cat.

What Became of Them?

He was a rat, and she was a rat,
  And down in one hole they did dwell,
And both were as black as a witch's cat,
  And they loved one another well.

He had a tail, and she had a tail,
  Both long and curling and fine;
And each said, 'Yours is the finest tail
  In the world, excepting mine.'

He smelt the cheese, and she smelt the cheese,
  And they both pronounced it good;
And both remarked it would greatly add
  To the charms of their daily food.

So he ventured out, and she ventured out,
  And I saw them go with pain;
But what befell them I never can tell,
  For they never came back again.

Pot Luck

Pot Luck

An epicure dining at Crewe,
Found quite a large mouse in his stew;
Said the waiter, 'Don't shout
And wave it about
Or the rest will be wanting one, too!'

There Was a Young Lady of Munich

There was a young lady of Munich,
Whose appetite was quite unich.
She contentedly cooed,
'There's nothing like food,'
As she let out a tuck in her tunich.

There Was a Young Lady of Rye

There was a young lady of Rye
With a shape like a capital 'I'.
When they said it's too bad,
She learned how to pad;
Which shows you that figures can lie.

The Pretty Young Thing

A pretty young thing from St Paul's
Wore a newspaper gown to a ball.
  The dress caught on fire
  And burned her attire
Front page, sporting section and all.

Rose

There was a young lady called Rose
Who had a large wart on her nose;
When she had it removed
Her appearance improved,
But her glasses slipped down to her toes.

Thin Flynn

There once was a skeleton named Flynn
Who looked quite remarkably thin,
  All bones, long and white,
  That rattled at night –
He should never have jumped out of his skin.

A Boy from Baghdad

There once was a boy from Baghdad,
An inquisitive sort of a lad.
  He said, 'I will see
  If a sting has a bee.'
And he very soon found that it had.

There Was a Young Student of Crete

There was a young student of Crete,
Who stood on his head in the street,
Said he, 'It is clear
If I mean to stop here
I shall have to shake hands with my feet.'

The New Gnu

There was a sightseer called Sue
Who saw a strange beast at the zoo.
  When she asked, ' Is it old?'
  She was smilingly told,
'It's not an old beast, but a gnu.'

There Was a Young Lady of Venice

There was a young lady of Venice,
Who used hard-boiled eggs to play tennis.
When they said, 'It seems wrong.'
She remarked, 'Go along!
You don't *know* how prolific my hen is!'

There Was a Young Fellow Named Hall

There was a young fellow named Hall
Who fell in the spring in the fall.
'Twould have been a sad thing
Had he died in the spring,
But he didn't – he died in the fall.

A Tone-Deaf Old Person of Tring

A tone-deaf old person of Tring,
When somebody asked him to sing,
Replied, 'It is odd,
But I cannot tell *God
Save the Weasel* from *Pop Goes the King.*'

An Eccentric Old Person from Slough

An eccentric old person from Slough,
Who took all his meals with a cow,
Always said, 'It's uncanny,
She's so like Aunt Fanny,'
But he never would indicate how.

Taken for a Ride

A major, with wonderful force,
Called out in Hyde Park for a horse.
  All the flowers looked round,
  But no horse could be found,
So he just rhododendron, of course.

A cat in Despondency

A cat in despondency sighed
And resolved to commit suicide.
  She passed under the wheels
  Of eight automobiles,
And under the ninth one she died.

christmas crackers

What Santa Needs for Christmas

When in frosty midnight,
He cruises through the air
What Santa needs for Christmas
Is fur-lined underwear.

While Shepherds Washed

While shepherds washed their socks by night
All seated round the tub,
A bar of pure white soap came down
And they began to scrub.

Good King Wenceslas (1)

Good King Wenceslas
Knocked a bobby senseless
Right in the middle of
Marks and Spencer's.

Good King Wenceslas (2)

Good King Wenceslas looked out
On a cabbage garden:
He bumped into a Brussels sprout
And said, 'I beg your pardon.'

We Three Kings of Orient

We three kings of Orient are,
One in a taxi, one in a car,
One in a scooter, blowing his hooter,
Following yonder star.

Lettuce Marry

Lettuce Marry

Do you carrot all for me?
My heart beets for you,
With your turnip nose
And your radish face.
You are a peach.
If we cantaloupe.
Lettuce marry;
Weed make a swell pear.

He Spoke the Truth

'Your teeth are like the stars,' he said
And pressed her hand so white.
He spoke the truth, for like the stars,
Her teeth came out at night.

Phoebe

A certain young chap named Bill Beebee
Was in love with a lady called Phoebe.
  'But,' said he, 'I must see
  What the licence fee be
Before Phoebe be Phoebe B. Beebee.'

I Love You

I love you, I love you,
I love you divine.
Please give me your bubble-gum,
You're *sitting* on mine.

Not a Word

They walked the lane together.
The sky was dotted with stars.
They reached the rails together,
He lifted up the bars.
She neither smiled nor thanked him,
Because she knew not how,
For he was only the farmer's boy
And she was the Jersey cow.

It's Hard to Lose Your Lover

It's hard to lose your lover
When your heart is full of hope
But it's worse to lose your towel
When your eyes are full of soap.

A Memorable Miss

I remember – I remember well –
The first girl that I kissed.
She closed her eyes. I closed mine.
And then – worst luck – we missed!

Dinner Date

'Twas in a restaurant they met,
Romeo and Juliet.
He had no cash to pay the debt
So Romeo'd while Juliet.

The Daughter of the Farrier

The daughter of the farrier
Could find no one to marry her,
Because she said
She would not wed
A man who could not carry her.

The foolish girl was wrong enough,
And had to wait quite long enough;
For as she sat
She grew so fat
That nobody was strong enough.

The Female Highwayman

Priscilla on one summer's day,
Dressed herself up in men's array;
With a brace of pistols by her side
All for to meet her true love she did ride.

And when she saw her true love there
She boldly bade him for to stand.
'Stand and deliver, kind sir,' she said,
'For if you don't I'll shoot you dead.'

And when she'd robbed him of all his store,
Said she, 'Kind sir, there's one thing more;
The diamond ring I've seen you wear,
Deliver that and your life I'll spare.'

'That ring,' said he, 'my true love gave;
My life I'll lose but that I'll save.'
Then, being tender-hearted like a dove,
She rode away from the man she love.

Anon they walked upon the green,
And he spied his watch pinned to her clothes,
Which made her blush, which made her blush
Like a full, blooming rose.

''Twas me who robbed you on the plain,
So here's your watch and your gold again.
I did it only for to see
If you would really faithful be.
And now I'm sure that this is true,
I also give my heart to you.'

Order in the court

Order in the court

Order in the court
The judge is eating beans
His wife is in the bath-tub
Counting submarines.

The owner of the Inside Inn

The owner of the Inside Inn
Was outside his Inside Inn,
With his inside outside his Inside Inn

The Couple from Fife

In a cottage in Fife
   Lived a man and his wife,
Who, believe me, were comical folk;
   For, to people's surprise,
   They both saw with their eyes,
And their tongues moved whenever they spoke!
   When quite fast asleep,
   I've been told that to keep
Their eyes open they could not contrive;
   And they walked on their feet,
   And 'twas thought what they eat
Helped, with drinking, to keep them alive!

A Peanut Sat on the Railroad Track

A peanut sat on the railroad track,
His heart was all a-flutter,
Along came a train –
Toot-toot! – peanut butter!

Busy Street

Sausage dog
Busy street
Motor car
Mince meat

Willie and the Hard Man

Willie, at a passing gent,
Threw a batch of fresh cement
Crying, 'Wait until you dry,
Then you'll be a real hard guy!'

The Gum-chewing Student

The gum-chewing student,
The cud-chewing cow,
Are somehow alike,
Yet different somehow.
Just what is the difference –
I think I know now –
It's the thoughtful look
On the face of the cow.

The Rain Makes All Things Beautiful

The rain makes all things beautiful,
The grass and flowers too.
If rain makes all things beautiful,
Why doesn't it rain on you?

Fatty, Fatty, Boom-a-Latty

Fatty, Fatty, Boom-a-latty;
This is the way he goes!
He is so large around the waist,
He cannot see his toes.

This is Mr Skinny Linny;
See his long lean face!
Instead of a regular suit of clothes,
He wears an umbrella case!

To be Answered in Our Next Issue

When a great tree falls
And people aren't near,
Does it make a noise
If no one can hear?
And which came first,
The hen or the egg?
This impractical question
We ask then beg.
Some wise men say
It's beyond their ken.
Did anyone ever
Ask the hen?

Imagine

If the sea was in the sky,
And trees grew underground,
And if all fish had giant teeth,
And all the cows were round;
If birds flew backwards all the time,
And vultures ruled the land,
If bricks poured down instead of rain,
If all there was was sand;
If every man had seven heads,
And we spoke Double Dutch,
And if the sun came out at night,
I wouldn't like it much.

Index of first lines

Index of first lines   171